ALLEN PHOTOG

C000234727

SADDLE FITTING

CONTENTS

AN HOLISTIC APPROACH

Good saddle fitting requires an holistic approach. Look at the whole horse, the type and build, the width across the chest, the amount of bone, the condition of the back and the musculature. Remember that horses, like humans (although not so obviously), change shape during their lifetime. Horses aged between 10 and 14 years get middle-age spread and may need a different fitting from the older horse. The young, newly broken horse needs a very comfortable saddle which allows him freedom to change shape.

This horse is a 16 hh four-year-old thoroughbred gelding. Looking at the musculature, you can see that he has not been using all his muscles correctly. He has no 'top line' yet. Working with a correctly fitting saddle should improve this outline within three months.

THE SADDLE

The saddle is the most important and expensive piece of equipment you will purchase for your horse. Not only will the horse be happier but he will perform better in a well-fitting saddle and the bond between horse and rider will strengthen.

PROBLEMS THE SADDLE CAN CAUSE

A saddle which does not fit can cause a variety of problems, from minor – shortening of stride, stiffness, hollowing and resisting – to major – bucking, bad temper, napping and rearing. If the saddle does not fit properly the horse uncharacteristically cannot give of his best.

Try to relate the horse's discomfort to your own. If he is asked to work in a saddle which is too small or tight, it is equivalent – in human terms – to wearing a coat a couple of sizes too small and being asked to do a handstand. If the saddle is too wide for the horse, it would be like you wearing slippers and going for a walk: comfortable in the short term but more and more uncomfortable as the walk progresses.

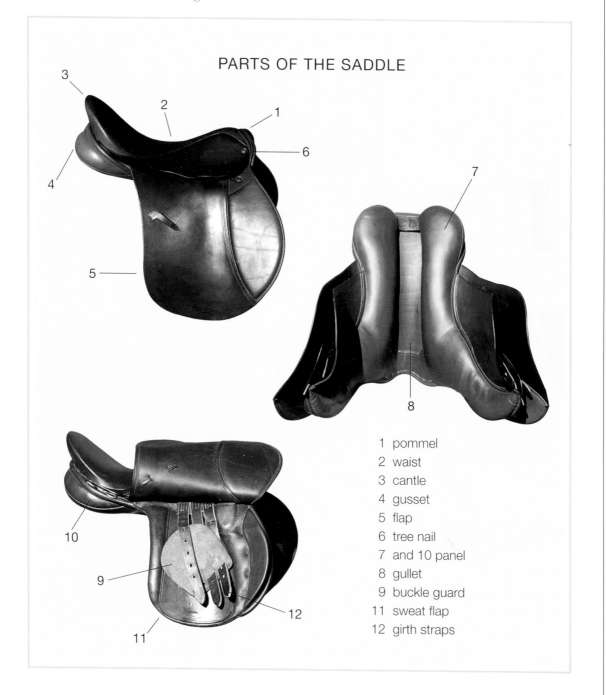

PARTS OF THE SADDLE

1 pommel
2 waist
3 cantle
4 gusset
5 flap
6 tree nail
7 and 10 panel
8 gullet
9 buckle guard
11 sweat flap
12 girth straps

Watch your horse moving free and unrestricted in the field. With care, he can move like this under saddle, provided the saddle fits (like the one on the right). If you have a definite problem with your horse, it is easier to understand the importance of the saddle's fit. However, many horses which seem to go well would in fact be transformed in athleticism, balance, elasticity and fluidity of gait if they had better fitting saddles. Most horses are very patient and suffer in silence!

Compare the fit down the front of the two saddles below. You can *see* where the one on the right does not fit.

> **REMEMBER**
>
> Badly fitting saddles hurt at worst; at best they are uncomfortable and restrict movement, and it is in these latter cases that it may not be obvious the horse is suffering.

THE HORSE'S BACK

The saddle has to give the horse full movement through his back. It must not prevent or inhibit the muscles of the shoulder and below the wither from expanding and contracting.

Horses must be able to use all their muscles easily, even under saddle, to ensure that the hocks can engage and produce lengthening. This allows the top line to develop. If the saddle pinches the horse's back it is physically impossible for the horse to work through into a natural outline, no matter what artificial aids – draw reins, side reins, strong bits, spurs – are used. The horse comes into shape from his hindquarters and not by being pulled in the mouth.

YOUR NEW HORSE

When you first get a horse, be aware of the fact that he is almost bound to change shape over the first few months. He may have a different routine, a change of diet, bedding and environment. All these things should be allowed to stabilise before fitting a new saddle. However, if you must get a new saddle immediately, be prepared for an alteration after a few months. Taking a wither pattern on a regular basis is always helpful. As well as measuring the horse's

SOME ANATOMY

There is an intricate muscle structure along the horse's back. Below the wither a 'junction box' of muscles works along each side of the spine and links up with other muscles on the diagonal as well.

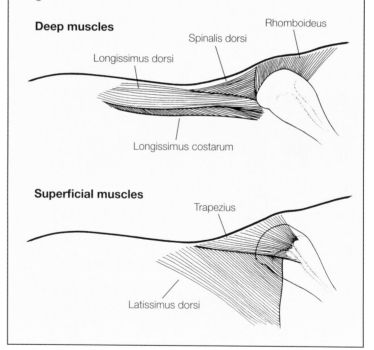

Deep muscles

Rhomboideus
Spinalis dorsi
Longissimus dorsi
Longissimus costarum

Superficial muscles

Trapezius
Latissimus dorsi

shape, remember that horses, like humans, can sometimes differ from left to right. A saddle fitted to the horse's exact shape can 'block' the natural build up of muscle. A symmetrical, balanced saddle is vital.

TAKING A WITHER PATTERN

Make sure the horse is standing square and level. Use a 'flexi-curve' which can be bought from a stationer or art shop. Standing on the nearside, place the centre of the flexi-curve over the top of the wither and feel round the shoulder, then press the curve down behind the shoulder. Ask someone to hold the top of the curve while you go round and repeat the procedure on the offside. Take it off carefully, lay it on a piece of paper, and draw round the underside. Later you can make a cardboard template from the paper shape.

AUTHOR'S TIP

If your horse's wither pattern resembles the one shown here, the muscles have wasted and he needs sympathetic saddling to allow the muscles to redevelop. You will need padding initially to make a saddle fit (see later section on padding and numnahs).

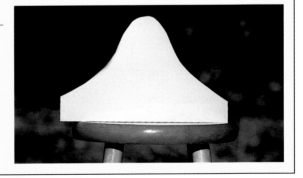

USING THE WITHER PATTERN

Place the saddle on a stool with the front extending over the edge, and hold up the template. If it fits, the template should fit snugly into the saddle, giving three fingers clearance into the pommel. The widest part should not be restricted. Better still, ask someone to help you by holding the saddle while you hold the template.

DESIGN OF THE SADDLE

You may want a saddle for jumping, dressage, cross-country, long distance or general purpose; the shape will differ in detail, but the principles of fitting as far as the horse's back is concerned remain the same.

The shape and size of a saddle is based on the tree, which is usually made of beechwood. Trees are made in width-fittings – normally narrow, medium and wide (see below) – and in different lengths. We are only offered three standard widths irrespective of whether the horse is a Shetland, a Thoroughbred or a Shire! Some companies do make, or will make to a wither pattern, in-between widths, which is a step forward.

The arrows on the tree shown here indicate width (1) and the 'point' (2).

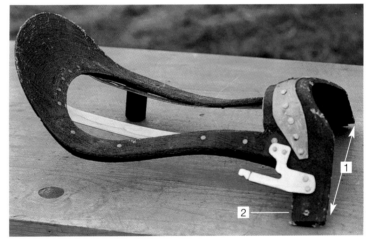

SYMMETRY

This is most important. Stand your saddle on end so that you can line up the centre of the cantle with the centre of the pommel to check that the tree is not twisted.

Turn the saddle upside down and check the panels are straight and not too firmly stuffed. Again, check the symmetry. The saddle below is too stuffed and lumpy and the panels are asymmetrical.

SHAPE

Think about your horse's spine and the way the saddle must rest on either side of it. Obviously, a big bearing surface, either side of the gullet will be the most comfortable.

The gullet should be about $2\frac{1}{2}$ in (6 cm) wide along the full length of the saddle, flaring out at the front. You should be able to run three fingers' width the entire length of the gullet (see above right).

A soft, smooth panel, free of lumps (which could cause pressure points) will spread the rider's weight. There should be some 'give' in the panel, which should be flat, not banana-shaped, so that you get an even pressure right along the back. The horse's muscles must be able to work into the panel – hence the importance of not stuffing the panels too tightly (see below right, where the panels are too firm).

It is important, however, that the saddle gullet should not be *too* wide. The further from the spine the saddle sits, the greater the risk of bruising on the weaker muscle.

WARNING

Too narrow a gullet design of many otherwise good quality saddles can damage the muscles along the spine; the hard rounded panels of some saddles give the effect of the rider sitting on two rolling pins on either side of the horse's spine.

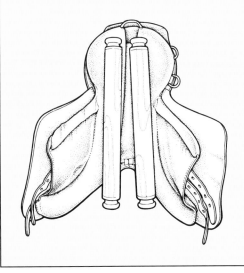

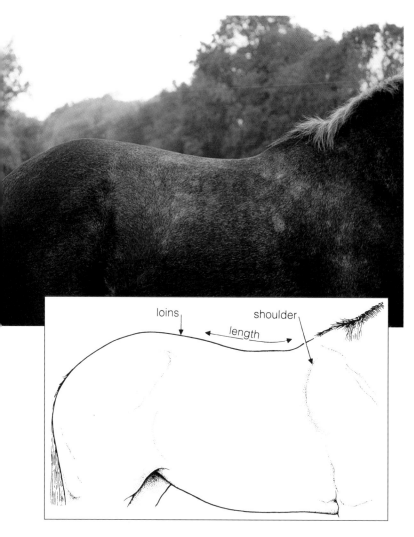

loins

shoulder

length

SIZE

Saddles are sold by width and length. The width must fit the horse; the length must fit the horse as well as you. It must be short enough to fit *behind* the scapula (shoulder blade) with enough clearance in front of the loins. If you have a short-backed horse, you can either have a saddle made with a slightly shorter panel or find one with a straight head.

For example, if *you* need a 17 in (43 cm) saddle, but it is slightly too long on your horse's back, ask your saddler about a 16 ½ in (42 cm) one with a straight head, which will allow more room in the seat for the rider. The saddle length is normally measured from the centre of the tree nail to the centre of the cantle.

Please don't compromise your horse; different saddle makers have different solutions to this problem.

AUTHOR'S TIP

Length of flap is important too, especially for short adults or children. We sometimes see a child trying to 'put a leg on' when the leather saddle flap comes down to their ankle (see left)!

FITTING A SADDLE

The most important point to concentrate on when fitting a saddle is the width. Many people put a saddle on a horse, check that it clears the withers and are satisfied. But a saddle can clear the withers and be much too tight. Think about the width of the horse's chest, imagining a point about 6 in (15 cm) below the wither – this is the width to guide the fit.

It is always better to have a slightly wider saddle and add flock to the wither area, (rather than one which is too tight), thus allowing the horse to work through his back and free the shoulder movement. The pressure of a too tight saddle either side of the wither is comparable to a belt which is too tight for you.

Both of these saddles are too tight. In the photograph on the right you can *see* the wrinkle where it is pinching. The saddle shown below is sitting too high up above the wither.

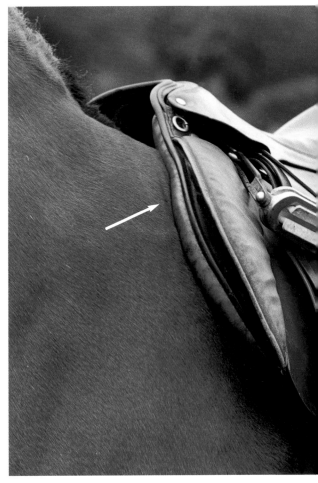

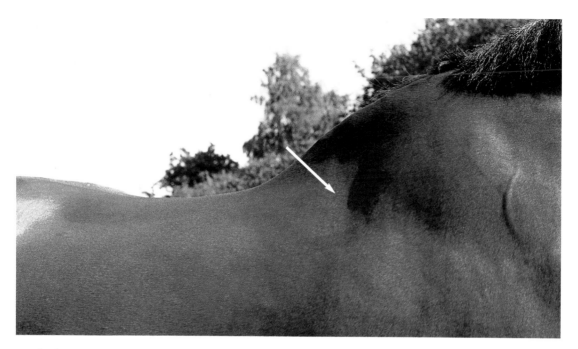

If a horse has been wearing a saddle for a long time which is too tight on each side of the wither, he will have deep hollows in the 'junction box' area where the muscle should be (see above).

A saddle which is wide enough to allow a horse to develop the muscle in this area would initially be too low on the withers because it would not yet have muscle to support it. And a saddle which *appeared* to fit would not allow for muscle development. So if the horse's shape is wrong, it is important not to fit to that wrong shape, or the situation will not get any better. This is where padding may help initially. But expert help should be sought in such a case; a saddle which is too wide will still be too wide, *even when the horse is properly muscled* and should not be padded to try to make it fit. The padding is a temporary remedial measure (see later section on numnahs).

It is equally essential that the saddle, once fitted at the front, should sit *all along* the horse's back. To test this, girth the saddle on the first and third girth straps to anchor the saddle from front to back. If the saddle lifts at the back, the horse probably needs a saddle with either a deeper gusset or a panel that is flatter in the waist.

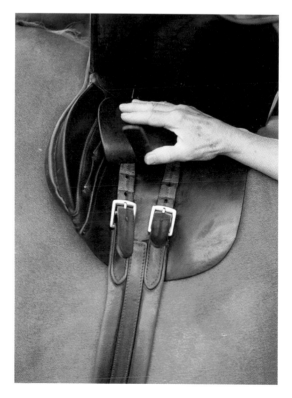

POSITIONING

The positioning of the saddle on the horse's back is very important. Most people put saddles on *too far forward* (see above). To find the correct position, place the saddle gently in front of the wither and slide it back. It normally finds its own resting place but, to check, put the hand against the shoulder and feel for the scapula. The saddle must sit behind this. By having the saddle in the correct position, the horse will have a longer stride and feel lighter in the hand.

To make sure that the saddle does not go too far back, put your hand next to the whorls which indicate the position of the loins. There should be at least 6 in (15 cm) clearance between the back of the saddle and the whorls. Use the width of a hand plus 1 in as a rough guide.

THINK!

If your saddle is too far forward and sitting *on* the shoulder, the saddle will twist from left to right across the spine as each shoulder moves. At the same time, the horse has to lift the saddle, *and* you *and* stretch the girth on *every* stride.

When the saddle is in the correct position, check that the seat of the saddle is horizontal to the ground. If it is tipped backwards, the balance of the saddle throws the rider's weight to the back of the saddle, thus creating undue pressure and bruising in the sacro-iliac region (the loins).

If the pommel is too high (see below left), the saddle may be too narrow, and the rider will be riding 'uphill'. This might also indicate that the saddle is too far forward. If the pommel is too low (see below right), either the saddle is too wide, needs reflocking, or the horse needs to build muscle and the front needs padding until it does so.

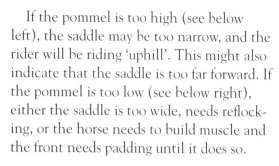

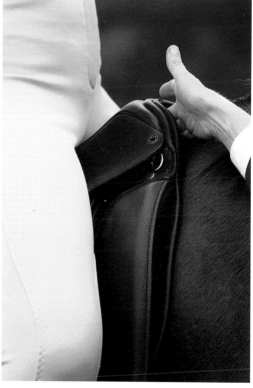

A saddle should fit behind the shoulder blades (leaving free movement of the shoulders) not *on* the shoulders. There should be a finger's width between the shoulders and the saddle.

In this position, the saddle should not normally allow more than three fingers' clearance over the wither *when the rider is in the saddle*. More than this may indicate a too narrow saddle.

If the saddle is tipped for-
wards and has little room
under the pommel, then it
needs to be lifted. A reputable saddler should, in this
instance, drop out the panel
and feather the flock down
the knee rolls and along the
panel to graduate the flocking and smooth any lumps.
A wadge of flock stuffed just
in the front of the saddle
will only cause discomfort to
the horse.

When the saddle is in
place and girthed, feel down
the side from the wither and
see if you can bring your
fingers through easily. There
should be no blockages.

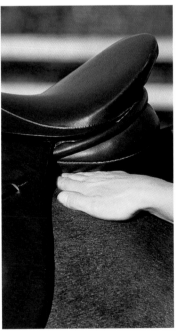

Then place your hand palm down under the
sweat flap up to the stirrup bar area and pull
gently backwards under the line of the
saddle. (That is, with the panel sitting on top of your fingers and the underneath of
your fingers running along the horse's back.)
Your hand should feel an even pressure
along the entire length without blocking.

NUMNAHS AND PADS

Sometimes, by getting the width right, we lose the height between the pommel and the horse, and that is where we may need to make use of numnahs and wither pads – at least until the horse has built up enough muscle to lift the saddle away from the wither. Many people have a saddle reflocked if it seems too low over the wither. This can just make it very tight and actually *prevent* the muscle developing on either side of the wither. It is better to use temporary padding until the muscle builds up in the 'junction box' area. It is in this area where the muscles must be free to move.

If the saddle is lifted a fraction, the rider can feel the tension disappear between the shoulder and the saddle, and one way to lift the saddle is by using a numnah. The best type is one similar to the old-fashioned pure wool felt numnah, which does not compress and yet still allows the horse full movement.

The fit of the numnah is almost as important as the fit of the saddle! If you are wearing well-fitting shoes but your socks are wrinkled, then you can still be sore and restricted! Natural fabrics are better for your horse. Numnahs can be bought in cotton quilting, sheepskin or wool. They must be big enough for the saddle to sit on them, with a good clearance all around so that there are no pressure points caused by 'turns', edges or securing straps.

Numnahs must be pulled right up into the gullet back and front, and the wither pad must not interfere with the panel of the saddle; it must be well clear. Really well-designed numnahs and saddle cloths are always shaped across the back and will therefore not press down on the horse's back.

AUTHOR'S TIP

When the saddle fits and the horse is well muscled, there is no real need for a numnah.

When trying to improve a horse's shape, or when the saddle is too low because the horse needs to build muscle, a pad is useful to give height over the withers and allow the muscles to expand and contract. Sometimes the saddle will need to be padded at the front only. For a horse with very deep hollows (caused by a poorly fitting saddle) use a wither pad and the muscle will start to develop. Gradually use thinner numnahs, until the horse's muscle is carrying the saddle up, and it no longer needs a pad.

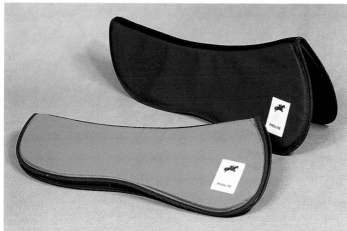

If a horse has no top line at all, or has any existing back problems, the new Prolite saddle pads are ideal; they are a mixture of gel and foam.

These pads can be used for general work, as well as jumping and eventing because, in normal use, the pads can prevent any jarring of the horse's back caused by the rider landing badly or heavily on his back.

A correctly fitting saddle will improve the musculature of even an older horse. This horse is an 18 year-old 16.2 hh Thoroughbred cross, shown before using a correctly fitting saddle, then three months and six months after using a correctly fitting saddle. See how the hollows in the 'junction box' area are beginning to fill out.

The horse before using a correctly fitting saddle…

the horse
3 months later…

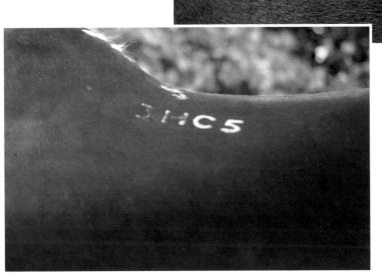

and 6 months later.

GIRTHS

The most common girths are the shaped soft leather ones, some with elastic ends, leather threefold, balding, webbing, foam-filled nylon or cotton, string and dressage.

Leather girths, if kept soft and supple, are the most comfortable for the horse. Where there is elastic on one side, this is for the horse's comfort and not for *your* benefit! The elastic should always be done up on the *off*side and, when the rider is in the saddle, the girth should only be tightened on the *near*side. This allows the horse to breathe. If you tighten the elastic side from on top, two things will happen; one is that it is likely you will overtighten the girth and the second is that by stretching the elastic you will in fact pull the saddle over to that side.

> ## HORSE COMFORT
>
> Remember that your horse must be allowed to breathe, and that the girth shouldn't be so tight that you can't get a hand between horse and girth comfortably when the rider is on top.

Beware of some nylon and cotton girths, which can sometimes allow the saddle to slip. If in doubt, use a girth sleeve, making sure that any seam is to the outside.

Be careful with dressage girths. Sometimes, the very long straps, designed for the rider's comfort, can cause discomfort to the horse by allowing the buckle to come into contact with his elbow (see below).

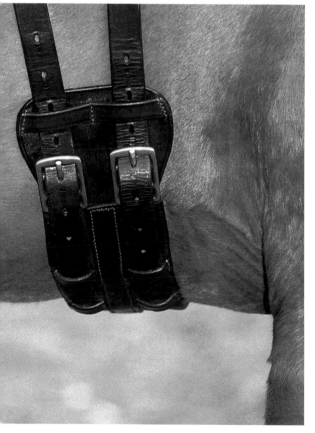

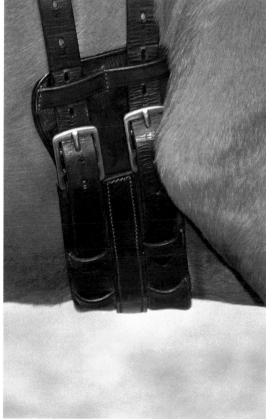

SECOND-HAND SADDLES

Buyer beware! If buying from any other source than a reputable saddler, please make sure firstly that the saddle is sound. It is well worth paying a saddler to check the points below.

CHECK

- that the tree is sound and symmetrical – that is, not broken or twisted;

- that the girth webs and stitching are in good order;

- that the rivets in the head of the tree are all intact;

- that the stirrup bars are symmetrically aligned.

Make sure that the leather is soft and pliable but not too heavy: heaviness can be caused by too much oiling, which the wool flock inside the panel can soak up. This tends to make the panel lumpy and uncomfortable (see right).

Having established that your second-hand saddle is good and sound, then the fitting of the saddle should be the same as for a new one, but there are a few additional procedures. Again, relate the horse's comfort to your own. Imagine someone wearing a pair of shoes over at the heels. If you wore them, you would have to have them re-heeled, or you too would start walking over on your heels. When you buy or acquire a second-hand saddle (even if it is from your own last horse), have it re-balanced so that your horse is starting with a perfectly aligned saddle. There are many reasons for saddles to need realignment prior to use. Horses usually work better on one rein than another, riders do not always sit squarely; all this affects the saddle shape – often imperceptibly – even if the saddle looks little used.

It is tempting to compromise on the fit of a second-hand saddle – especially if it is in good condition and a bargain! Don't! Treat the sizing as you would with a new one. Never take the flocking out to make the saddle wider; you risk exposing the points of the tree in such a way that the horse may feel them through the panel.

IMPORTANT

Measure and fit a second-hand saddle in just the same way as you would a new one. Take a wither pattern. If the saddle does not fit, do not buy it.

Look at the back of a horse that has never had a saddle on. No lumps, white hairs, hollows, wasted muscle. We do not have to damage our horses' backs. After wearing a saddle which fits perfectly, your horse can look and move as he would have done in the wild.

ACKNOWLEDGEMENTS

The Saddle Fitting Centre, Walsall; Norton and Newby,
Old Beaconsfield; Tracey Hawkins; Ann Lewis; Lisa Moore;
Joanna Scrivens

British Library Cataloguing-in-Publication Data.
A catalogue record for this book is available from the
British Library

ISBN 0.85131.708.1

First published in Great Britain 1998
J.A. Allen
Clerkenwell House
Clerkenwell Green
London EC1R 0HT

Design and Typesetting by Paul Saunders
Edited by Susan Beer
Series editor Jane Lake
Colour Separation by Tenon & Polert (H.K.) Ltd
Printed by Gutenberg Press Limited, Malta